Ordered Steps

A Testimony of Prophetic

Synchronicity

Mike Killion

Ordered Steps:
A Testimony of Prophetic Syncronicity

By Mike Killion

Publication by:
NavProMedia
Charlotte, North Carolina

All Scripture quotations include a description of the translation or paraphrase used.

ISBN: 978-0-615-63583-5

Printed in the United States of America
First Printing

Recommendations

I met Mike Killion at his son Joel's church, *Frontlines School of The Spirit*, in Wilson, North Carolina about five years ago. Today we are the best of friends and I consider him as one of my mentors.

The contents of these pages are so important to me that I want them to be important to you. May the contents and the progression of this man's life grab your heart. The title of this book, Ordered Steps, comes from Psalm 37:23 which says, *"The steps of a good man are ordered of the Lord and He delights in his way.* When we consider the word "ordered" it means "to stand erect, set up, to adjust or fit or direct." The word "good" brings to mind Psalm 25:12, which says, *"Who then is the man who fears the Lord? He will instruct him in the way chosen for him."* The word "steps" in Psalm 37:23 means "his course of life, the way in which he goes.

The general idea is that the good man is the object of Divine favor and is under the care of God. I have had the great privilege of knowing Mike as a mentor, teacher, brother-in-Christ, and friend. I am a witness to the grace of God and the Holy Spirit directing his thoughts, affections, and designs in his life. I have seen the providence overruling events to make the way plain for him as he has been led step by step even when the final destination was afar off. He has embraced both the times of certainty and uncertainty when it seemed that God wasn't speaking. Bear in mind that Mike has been on his ordered journey for about 35 years. I want you to notice the patience he has been given like a marathon runner who perseveres and earns the prize.

The word "persevere" includes doing something in spite of the difficulty or delay in achieving success with glory as the final result. This is one of Mike's strongest attributes. His patient perseverance has influenced me richly to remain strong in my journey. This is what the author is to me.

Listen to Mike's testimony and consider the ways he has been led. HE can AND IS leading you also. Resolve to continue on in YOUR race for there are and will be many who will need your example as the Day comes to a conclusion and a new Day dawns.

Notice also how the author was the "big man on campus," which took him to the mountaintop of school popularity amongst his peers, but also confesses to the lows of disappointment and failure. God's people will go high, and they will go low. And, they will come out the other side just like my pal Mike Killion. What influences you? Is it the Kingdom of God and the training by the Lord, or is it your own designs that you have for YOUR life? Is Christ's sacrifice worth the cost of everything you will give up in being "transformed by the renewing of your mind?" (Romans) What world do you live in anyway?

Mike's journey demonstrates the ordered APPREHENDED LIFE. Mike's testimony demonstrates how, when God chooses someone to "be with Jesus" that sometimes

God has to bypass their minds and work a work unbeknownst to them so He can accomplish things that that person cant do for themselves or would buck up if they were cognizant of the operation. This is vital as we continue in our journeys for the message has always been,

"If anyone desires to come after me, let him deny himself, and take up his cross..." (Matthew 16:24)

If we are honest we will confess to feeling the same way as Mike felt many times. We can see our cross in his, and we can see our struggles in the life of Christ also as *"He was tempted in all points as we are."* Mike confesses the "pity party" and we have to confess ours. The honesty and transparency Mike displays in this book has given me courage to confess my self-centeredness. Notice that once he recognized his self-life getting in the way during a moment of true Godlike sanity, Mike built an altar of remembrance and went back to see what the Lord has done. In the coming judgments, this function of remembering the Lord's deliverances will go a long way in helping us keep our sanity for "in that day" the judgment day we are in now, *"men's hearts and minds shall fail them for fear for looking after the things that are come on the earth."* It will be and now is that encouraging yourself will keep you sane.

I find this passage from David's life to be applicable to Mike's. Its from 1 Samuel 30:6

"After returning home he found it had been burned with fire and the wives and children were carried off by the Amalekites."

The author has demonstrated the same resolve and heaven centeredness as David did. What's important to notice is that neither David nor Mike looked upon themselves for answers but rather encouraged themselves in the Lord. Mike goes on to compile key events in his life and in so doing sets a stage for you and I to do the same thing with the correct response. If we can learn some of these same lessons, we may be able to wisely do the right things when we are tested.

Keep an open mind and a teachable spirit. Allow the Holy Spirit to take us outside the boxes we have put ourselves in along the way as you read this book. By sharing our testimonies we can overcome the enemy of our souls.

Allow Mike Killion's testimony to encourage your faith and perhaps you have a book in you too.

Carolyn Steele
Fort Mill, SC

Inspiring!

That's what I can say about Mike's book, *Ordered Steps: A Testimony of Prophetic Synchronicity.*

I work with Mike at Reid's Gourmet Foods in Charlotte, North Carolina. As the Lord brought us to cross paths with each other, we had some good conversations about life and God long before he gave me the manuscript to read and reflect on. We talked about finding one's destiny and purpose in life. He offered that we will only find our purpose in God. He was so right by letting me read his book for it has led me to understand what God was really trying to tell me. I can't wait to read it again and get something else out of it.

K.B. Small

Charlotte, NC

Table of Contents

Introduction

"You have a book in you, dad."

That vision-setting statement came from my eldest son, Joel. We were having a discussion about my life and what God has done to me, for me, and through me in over thirty years. We were discussing phases of life, growth, and where we have come from, where we are now, and where God may be taking us next. I believe this is how prophetic people often think.

It was sometime in 2009 when we had this talk and I was confessing my true feelings of disappointment over my life. I guess many people experience this same thing, but I have come to realize that these feelings are a true indicator of our own self-centeredness and introspection. That is one sure way to depress one's self because most humans feel they have screwed things up and fallen short. (You know, it's the old mid-life crisis thing, when you feel you haven't accomplished what you wanted to.)

So, I was having one of these days and Joel was privy to it. I am glad I can admit my weaknesses to my two sons, Joel and Tyler, now in their thirties.

I was asking myself questions like, *What have I accomplished? What will I be remembered for? What kind of testimony will I leave behind to benefit my family and friends? What will they write on my tombstone?*

All these questions are valid. But what if we are truly the

generation that sees the return of Jesus? We will not die. We will receive our immortal bodies and keep on walking in an endless life. We will continue on in our quest for our destiny and live happier lives not subject to the injustices and weaknesses of a fallen world. Think of that. That's encouraging don't you think?

A Step Back...

I was a pretty good athlete when I was younger and was what they call a B.M.O.C., or "big man on campus." The attention and accolades were nice. I ate it up and used my "fame" to influence and control people. It was nice to be somebody's hero even if it was in something as insignificant as a ballgame. I grew up with a sense of overblown self importance.

Then, it all came crashing down with graduation. I became "average," whatever that is. I had to learn to live without the positive affirmation of my peers and live with only the support of my immediate family. (Sheesh, how boring is that?)

Men need to think that they are accomplishing something. We need a giant to bring down, a dragon to slay, or a mountain to climb. We need projects! Why? Because "an idle mind is the Devil's workshop." Men seem to need something to accomplish, but then, don't we all? Men need to think that they are conquering something – That is what we do – but instead I settled into the "boring" life of marriage, work, kids, paying bills, sitting on a pew at church, and whatever amusements I could find.

As I got older, doing "exploits" became rarer. I would ask, "What have I done for me lately? What have I done to be proud of? Anybody can do what I'm doing. There's no challenge in living this life. There's nothing special in what I'm doing. I want to be special." And really, don't you want to be special too? I mean really. R-e-a-l-l-y?!

I Wasn't Wrong

Now that I have been a Christian for about 35 years, I have learned that God created us to be special, to take dominion, to occupy until He comes, and to "make disciples of all nations." I am now 64 and I often ask myself, "What have I occupied, taken dominion over, or accomplished? What have I done to demonstrate that the Lord has been with me? What have I done to bring glory to Him and make Him say, 'Well done good and faithful servant?'"

When we go to church we hear plenty of testimonies from "model" Christians who share what great things God has done for them, in them, and through them. We hear what a "wonderful" life they are experiencing and then the "have-nots" in the pew are left to feel inadequate not realizing they are supposed to be inspire by what they are hearing.

This was just how I was feeling that day when Joel said to me out of the blue, "You have a book in you, dad."

"Me?" I said.

"Yes, you have a book in you! Look at all you have come through! Look at what the Lord has shown you! Look at what the Lord has done through you!"

That led to a cheerleading session where my son led the

cheers. He began to outline just some of the "exploits" that he was aware of. He began to remind me of the ordering that has taken place in my life over three decades.

As Psalm 37:23 says, "The steps of a [good] man are directed and established by the Lord…"

Isaiah 30:21 says, "And your ears will hear a word behind you, saying, This is the way; walk in it, when you turn to the right hand and when you turn to the left."

And finally, Psalm 68:33 says, "[Sing praises] to Him Who rides upon the heavens, the ancient heavens; behold, He sends forth His voice, His mighty voice."

I was having a pity party that day and the voice of my son made me recount what the Lord had done in and through me especially when it came to the people I've helped and effected. I had forgotten what the Lord had done. This is a common mistake many people make. We are taught to be humble and deflect the glory of man but in so doing we bury what the Lord has done and we forget; and this leads to depression; the type of depression I was feeling that day. Doesn't the Bible say that David encouraged himself in the Lord? I had discouraged myself through false humility and false humility is evidence of a religious spirit. It's a demon!

No wonder I was disoriented and disappointed. I had built an altar of remembrance when I wrote in my prophetic journal but I hadn't gone back to read it and encourage myself. God commanded the Israelites in the Old Testament to build altars all around Israel so they could teach their children what the Lord had done in times past so they would not get discouraged. I had gotten discouraged.

My son said, "You have a book in you dad. Just sit down with your journal and start outlining your life. Start compiling the events and instances of your life and go with the flow that comes."

So, I did what Joel said. I followed the advice of someone half my age and did what he told me. I didn't think I had anything worth saying but, after twenty minutes of meditating and jotting notes I had created a compilation of twenty-one interventions of God in my life, a table of contents, and the title *Ordered Steps*. Since finishing the manuscript in late 2011, I have had some tremendous and awe inspiring interventions that I will put in my second book, *Ordered Steps II*.

My purpose in writing this book is twofold:

1. To build an alter of remembrance for my children and their children so they will not feel alone in this life and will feel like they are a part of an ongoing "master plan" that God has laid on our family.

2. To teach principles that God is using in His dealings with us that may not be taught in the churches, or have been dealt with only in a shallow manner since there is "a famine in the land…for hearing the words of the Lord." (Amos 8:11b)

If you get anything out of this book, then it will have served its purpose. I am a strong believer that Divine revelation is like an onion; it comes in layers and the surface layer, while it has a small purpose and is beautiful, does not contain the edible part which gets sweeter and sweeter as you go deeper into the core. We must get to the core, the deeper understandings. The surface-life of churchianity is not maturing the Saints. It's time to go deeper!

This book contains events in a life of one apprehended for the "high calling of God in Christ Jesus." There are surface principles to be grasped and then there are deeper principles awaiting the one who meditates and contemplates on what deeper truths lay under the surface. So, I strongly encourage you to read this book with a prayerful, contemplative mind and heart.

Chapter One

Einstein & Prophetic Synchronicity

On several occasions over my nearly four decades as a Spirit regenerated Christian I've done some reading in the field of science seeking to know more regarding the scientific basis of our faith. Several years ago, I ran across several books by scientists who are Christians to see what the latest research has uncovered on proving the existence of the unseen God.

I also found a video on the life of Albert Einstein. What I learned was that the theory of relativity opened the door to a great understanding of the unseen world or what has become known as "Multidimensional Reality" or the existence of a world of reality outside or above the four dimensions – length, breadth, height, and time – we live in as humans. The conclusion I made was that if there is a realm of measurable reality higher than the one we are living in, we could justify that there is a world or realm of existence we can't see but is real. This, I thought, was where God and the "principalities and powers in high places" existed. Science would be proving the Bible.

I had always been drawn to the debate between atheistic and Christian scientists as they battled over whether the universe had been created by an Intelligent Designer or had spontaneously generated. I discovered the writings of Dr. Hugh Ross and was led to his book, *Lights in the Sky & Little Green Men: A Rational Christian Look at UFOs and Extraterrestrials.* In this book he and his co-authors admit that there is something to some of the UFO reports and that some of these reports point to undismissable phenomena. So, the issue that there is a world above our own is a reality as I had learned in Scripture, and, for me, this is affirmed by the encounters I've had with this supernatural world throughout my life. As a Spirit-filled Christian this should be a regular occurrence and be accepted as normal.

Of course, this is not new to us who believe in the Higher Power of God. The Bible is full of accounts of people having "close encounters of a heavenly kind." It has only been in this advanced age of science that science has been discovering what has been there all along. The higher realm exists and has SUBSTANCE. That's right; substance. As spiritual beings who have a soul and live in a body, we are supposed to have these encounters and we are meant to have them. As we get a better handle on this knowledge we can and should look forward to having greater and more powerful experiences with this realm. Our knowledge and acquaintance with our spiritual abilities should bring us to say what Jesus Himself said, "…The Son can do nothing of Himself, but what He sees the Father do; for whatsoever He does, the Son does likewise." (John 5:19b) Here we see evidence of three things:

1. Communication with the unseen

2. Synchronicity with the unseen

3. Partnership with the unseen

   So let it be with us, "On earth as it is in Heaven."

What is Prophetic Synchronicity?

Are these encounters with the unseen – with the supernatural realms – supposed to have meaning to us or have a pattern to them so we can discern a meaning to them? Are they just "happening" or are they just a reaction to fluctuations in our biochemistry, something we ate, or the phases of the moon?

Of course my thesis is that they have meaning. These events are happening to everyone because all humans are a creation of the Creator. If this Creator has created beings "after His kind," then His offspring have His nature and characteristics. When elephants make love, you get more elephants. When corn is planted you get more corn. When God planted His image in a new race in the earth, He got a crop of little "gods" as He reproduced Himself through the principle of reproduction He invented – after their kind. (See Genesis 1:24-26, Psalm 82:6, and John 10:34)

Like a good Father, He cares for us and provides for us. He has put into us all that He is and all that He has. Some of the gifts of His Spirit include wisdom, knowledge, discernment, and prophetic insight. As His children, we are able to hear and see what He is communicating to us on earth in the four dimensions we relate to everyday. Operating in this prophetic realm means we are not limited to the dimensions of earth. Isn't that how God created the first man, Adam, to live? Before the curse came, Adam was brilliant. He could communicate with the First Cause, his Creator. After the curse, he was relegated to using only a portion of his brain and was cut off from his Maker, his Friend. This resulted in imperfect knowledge which leads to confusion, which is our present condition.

We, as descendents of Adam suffer the same inability to live in direct fellowship with God, but our subconscious minds remember that we once did and man consciously hungers for restored fellowship. So we cry constantly, "Oh, God, where are you?" Even Karl Marx, an atheist, once said, "Man is incurably religious." "Something" inside us cries out for God.

Therefore, if we have this capacity to hear from heaven, and God made us to hear and fellowship with Him, and we are hearing from Him even if we don't realize it due to ignorance or busyness, is there any meaning or pattern to our supernatural encounters? Is there a reason we hear or is this just biochemistry we should be dismissing as coincidence?

What is in us?

Since God made us as a replica of Himself and we are His children, then we are supposed to be expressing Him throughout our lives. Just as our physical bodies grow from babyhood to adulthood, where we take on greater and greater responsibilities in this world, so will our spirit grow into a mature and responsible contributor to the Kingdom of God who possess the same attribute as the One who made us.

Let's see what He's given us:

1. The fruit of His Spirit – Love, joy, peace, patience, gentleness, faith, meekness, goodness, and temperance (Galatians 5:22,23).

2. The gifts of the Spirit – Wisdom, knowledge, faith, gifts of healings, working of miracles, prophecy, discernment of spirits, speaking in tongues, and interpretation of tongues (1 Corinthians 12). Romans 12:6 also mentions prophecy, ministry, teaching, exhortation, giving, administration (rulership, governing), and mercy.

3. The Seven Spirits of God – "…the Spirit of wisdom and understanding, the Spirit of counsel and might, the Spirit of knowledge and of the reverential and obedient fear of the Lord" (Isaiah 11:2).

4. Glory – What Jesus received from His Father was given to us (John 17:22). "And the glory which You gave to me, I have given to them, that they may be one even as we are one."

The result of this investment by our Father is prophetic synchronicity, which is another way of saying ordered steps. With all that has been given to us as the offspring of God, we have the privilege of living in communion with Him as we hear His voice and walk with Him, in His footsteps. This communion and fellowship will be necessary in the times ahead.

His Walk is Our Walk

Let's take a look at the close relationship Jesus had with

HIS Father.

So Jesus answered them by saying, I assure you, most solemnly I tell you, the Son is able to do nothing of Himself (of His own accord); but He is able to do only what He sees the Father doing, for whatever the Father does is what the Son does in the same way [in His turn]. The Father dearly loves the Son and discloses to (shows) Him everything that He Himself does. And He will disclose to Him (let Him see) greater things yet than these, so that you may marvel and be full of wonder and astonishment. I am able to do nothing from Myself [independently, of My own accord--but only as I am taught by God and as I get His orders]. Even as I hear, I judge [I decide as I am bidden to decide. As the voice comes to Me, so I give a decision], and My judgment is right (just, righteous), because I do not seek or consult My own will [I have no desire to do what is pleasing to Myself, My own aim, My own purpose] but only the will and pleasure of the Father Who sent Me. (John 5:19-20, 30)

Can you see now what has been given to you? Communion and fellowship with our Father Who made us and sent us into this world to do what He is doing. This kind of life is lived in synch with the greatest Power in the universe, the One who made the universe and all the scientific principles it operates within.

We are an extension of the Lord, living in union with Him. But, then, why do we mess up so much then? Why all the confusion and wasted steps? Why all the wasted time?

It is time for a revelation of who we are, of what we have, and of how to access it. Our quality of life depends on it and will depend on it in the coming "day of trouble" (Psalm 27:5; Nahum 1:7).

Einstein & Dr. Ross

I am an artist, a theologian and a writer. I am not a scientist. I'm not going to tell you all the scientific data uncovered by the brilliant men and women of science who have received revelations from God about the origin of the universe and how it works. I am thoroughly convinced that men don't discover scientific facts on their own. There have been many instances where researchers have been seeking an answer to a question and after coming to the end of themselves God dropped the answer on them.

This was the case with Einstein. One day he said, "I want to know how God created this world...I want to know His thoughts. The rest are details."[1] Later, after making this confession, the theory of relativity "dropped" into his mind.

The Theory of Relativity as laid out in Einstein's famous formula, E=mc2, opened the door to further understanding. It laid the groundwork for what we know today and what we know today can be summed up in a statement that Steven Hawking has

---

[1] Einstein, Albert. *World Year Of Physics: Einstein In The 21st Century.* N.p., n.d. Web. 24 Apr. 2012. <www.physics2005.org/einstein.html>.

made: "In real time, the universe has a beginning. Almost everyone now believes that the universe, and time itself had a beginning at the big bang."[2] Although he later retracted his statement the damage to his image had already been done. The cat was already out of the bag on what he really believed but wouldn't speak widely.

Also, I learned that thoughts and ideas have substance. Didn't I already know that? Isn't God called the "Logos" or Divine mind? Before He spoke the world into existence He must have had the thought to do it? After all, if I'm a replica of Him and I cut my grass on occasion, it all begins with the idea to do it. The thought is translated into energy and the energy is given to me to get out there and crank-up the mower. Without a thought there is no motivation which is e-n-e-r-g-y.

Therefore, energy is translated from the God-head, through the multiple dimensions that Einstein discovered, down from the highest realms of energy to the lowest forms which are where we live. Originally, as it relates to our move toward the fulfillment of our destiny, the thought that comes to our mind to accomplish a particular task comes from God's Spirit who is the comforter and the helper. Haven't you ever needed help remembering something, forgotten it, and then felt the nudge or prompt from somewhere outside you that caused the forgotten thought to come to mind? I have often left the house in the morning forgetting something and heard a voice in my head,

---

[2] *Why I Am a Christian* by Norm Geisler and Paul Hoffman.

"You forgot your lunch!" Do you think this is just coincidence or my own mind power? No, *my mind* forgot my lunch. Yes, you could say that this power is just the power of my mind since others have developed their minds to do such things. But, it is my understanding that God gave us a mind like His, then told us "...*Be ye transformed by the renewing of your mind*" (Romans 12:2), and finally gave us the gifts of wisdom, knowledge, discernment, and prophetic vision. People who have developed their mind power without the Holy Spirit can still enjoy these powers because these people were originally born with a destiny in God and "*the gifts and calling of God are without repentance*" (Romans 11:29)' in other words, even if we stray away from our calling through folly, God still has this power reserved for you.

So, again, thoughts have substance. Selah (Think on this)

Chapter Two

The Weather & I

Disclaimer:

I can see how someone would read my experiences and how I speak of them and say that I really have a high opinion of myself - that I am "special." Well, I must tell you that I may be just a tad guilty of such a charge but not because I am special but because I am yielded and I allow God to have His way in my life.

I was born under the curse; spiritually deaf, dumb, blind, and mentally and emotionally unbalanced compared to the mind God wants to give us. Then in my early twenties, the light bulb went on after I surrendered to the Creator's wooing and He started to remake me as I yielded to His daily lessons. Once this happened, God began to synchronize my life through ordered steps.

The Apostle Paul taught us that we can boast in only one thing and that is what God has done in us, through us and to us. This "bragging" must be done in such a way that it glorifies God. Whenever someone is heard "bragging" on what God has done, it sometimes follows that someone else feels pangs of jealousy. I am surely not meaning to make anyone jealous, but if that does happen I am encouraging them to gain strength from my testimony to inspire them to realize that what happens to others can be yours too. All that is needed is to follow in

Yeshua's footsteps, making Him your example and not men.

Shortly after moving to Charlotte, NC, from Wilson, North Carolina, my mother died and I received my inheritance. I used it to build a house and pay it off. At that time I had a sense within me that God was setting me up to be in a secure position when the grand-daddy of all financial crashes happened as spoken of in the Book of Revelation.

So, the house was built, but I needed a lawn to guard against erosion. I had spent all my money on the house and had to buy the grass seed out of pocket from my weekly paychecks. I didn't have enough money for topsoil or hay. I just sowed the seed on low quality soil that was 80-90% clay. A young man who had landscaping experience in his family business was renting a room in my house. He said the seeds wouldn't grow and if they did it they would burn out in the summer time because there would be no deep root system.

At this time the ground was dried up clay and had cracks in it. All the time, I had it in my mind that I was going to sow seed on this bad soil, disregarding the soil composition. I had to cultivate the dried up soil somehow and was willing to get out there with a hoe and crunch it up because I couldn't afford a tiller. Soon, after I found that the soil was too hard, I asked God for a miracle. Later that week, it rained for three days and then a cold front came in and froze the soil down about five inches. Well, as you may know, ice expands and when it did it loosened up the soil down five inches when it thawed a week later. That's when I sowed the seed and it came up as the temps warmed up. I had grass against all odds.

But the young man was right in that when the summer heat came the grass began to get brown. So I prayed, *"Oh, Father, don't let my grass die. I need rain in this drought time."* Then, the Lord spoke to my mind and said, *"Speak to the rain; call it down yourself!"* So, I called to the rain and commanded it to come as if it were a little child. It hadn't rained in over six weeks and the temperatures during the daytime was topping ninety-five degrees. Everything was turning brown, including my nature defying grass. But that changed when, in eight hours, a deluge of rain came down and turned every brown thing green again.

This went on for the next 7-8 years. I still have not put any topsoil on my lawn but I have fertilized to control weeds. And about thirteen straight times, in 7-8 years, when I called for rain, I got rain! But, here's what the Lord taught me through this: When you dedicate your life in full to the Lord to serve Him and you keep a consistent prayer life, *you become His friend and He shares His thoughts with you*. I call it the "V Formation" because, as with geese in flight, the Holy Spirit becomes the lead goose as we fly *in formation* with Him. What He does, we do. He loves it that way.

Calming the Wind

A few years later, I had a twenty-four foot by eighteen

foot shed built on a concrete slab. I designed it to have a twenty foot ceiling because I wanted to build a loft for storage. The builder set up eight-by-eight treated posts and the frame out of two-by-sixes and two-by-fours. But he did something strange. He didn't sink the posts in concrete. He set them on top of the concrete and used L-brackets and bolts to secure them. I didn't like this method.

One night, after the frame was about 75% up, a rain-storm came in, preceded by a strong wind for about thirty minutes. It was near hurricane strength. I saw the frame structure moving in the wind and feared it would collapse. I thought about calling the builder so he could come out and take more precautions to secure it. But, the Lord spoke. He said, "Calm the wind!" So, I began to speak to the wind. I began to do everything I had learned to do from the prayer-manuals over the space of sixty seconds.

Before I even spoke "In the Holy name of Jesus!" the wind had died down to almost nothing. This windstorm had been blowing for thirty to forty-five minutes at near hurricane force and within ten seconds after praying about 45 seconds, it stopped almost instantly.

"Wow!"I thought. "Oh God, what are you doing here? What are you showing me?" He impressed on me, "I'm trying to show you that you have power in your voice when you speak in My Spirit." This changed my life and how I spoke to people. Then, I heard in my mind these words, *"You have heard it said that 'When E.F. Hutton speaks, people listen,' but I say to you,*

'When Mike Killion speaks, people listen." After that, I began to notice over the next four to five months that when I spoke to people, they were not ignoring me but listening and changing what they believed because of what I spoke to them.

Authority is a gift. So is the power of persuasion. It should be used for the Kingdom. I didn't do anything to change my communication style. To me, I talk the same way I always have, but the Bible says, "*Faith comes by hearing and hearing by the Word of God.*" When you speak His Word to someone, He uses you in spite of you. They hear what He wants them to hear and you may not be aware of anything that is going on.

In the days of great shaking and trouble there will be such desperation in so many people that those of us who exhibit the love, joy, peace, patience, gentleness, kindness, temperance, and self control of God will be sought after. Many will want what we have. This condition is even now beginning to happen. Can you see it?

Chapter Three

Fellowshipping with Cardinals

In 1971, I married my dream girl, Sharon Engeldinger of Olive Street in Milwaukee. Within three years we were changed by God's Spirit. It was the mid-70s when we followed the Lord to Springfield, Missouri to go to Bible school so we could prepare for the mission field. We had to sell the condo we had just bought and had to make enough money to make the trip to our new home. We also wanted a place where we could take our cat with us.

When we went to Springfield to search for a job for Sharon and an apartment, a job was secured quickly for Sharon and when we went to look at the apartment on Battlefield Road, the apartment manager opened the door only to reveal a cat sitting at her feet. We knew this was the place for us and that we were experiencing divinely ordered steps.

Wilson

We were not there very long before we "sensed" the Lord was leading us out of Missouri to Wilson, North Carolina, where a prophet had a church. This prophet had a signs and wonders ministry we had not yet seen in our young Christian experience.

We spent several weeks seeking the Lord for a definite leading that we were to go to North Carolina. One day we received a phone call from this man as we were having dinner with some friends talking about whether we should move to Wilson. In that call he told us that he "saw" us having dinner and that the topic of conversation at the table was whether we should move to Wilson. We were amazed and realized that if we were ever to come into this level of Spirit lead communication we would have to sit under the man who had made this level of anointing a way of life.

The final confirmation came one day when I called Sharon during my lunch break at my job. I was working for another prophet, Bill Britton, as the administrator of his *Voice of The Overcomer* correspondence school. Sharon interrupted our conversation when a red cardinal came and sat on the railing of our small balcony outside our patio door on the second floor. She said it seemed that the cardinal was looking at her and that he wouldn't move. She was sitting on the couch just inside the patio door window and was actually about four to five feet from the bird. She said that the event was "strange" since it sat there and looked at her for such a long time. We knew this was Missouri's state bird, but I asked her if she knew what the state bird of North Carolina was. She said she would look it up in the encyclopedia when we got off the phone. She did and when she saw that the state bird of Missouri (You know, the St. Louis Cardinals?) was also the state bird of North Carolina, she called me right back. I said something like, "Okay, that confirms it. We're moving to North Carolina." Immediately, we started to make arrangements.

On our trip to North Carolina, I was driving the Ryder

truck and was in front of Sharon in our car. As we came across the Tennessee/North Carolina border on I-40, a cardinal flew across the hood of the truck; it was so close to the window I could have reached out and grabbed it. I slowed down, pulled over to the shoulder, and stopped the truck. Sharon stopped behind me. I got out and told her of the incident and said it was a confirmation that we were in the right place at the right time. We know it now as prophetic synchronicity – otherwise known as *ordered steps*.

Chapter Four

Brushes with Death

I have had three brushes with death in my life time.

1. At six years old, I met a car in Montreal, Quebec, Canada
2. Swimming on my honeymoon
3. Heading for the swamp

I Met a Car in Montreal

My father took a year-long assignment with his company who needed a man to live in Montreal for a year. So we moved from Milwaukee. I was six years old and couldn't attend school because the first grade teacher could not speak English. French was the native tongue, therefore, I sat out of school that whole year.

Hockey was the national sport and there was a rink across the street from our duplex. My brother Norm, who was five years older than me was playing hockey across the street one Saturday and I decided I wanted to go over and watch the game. My mother bundled me up in many layers of clothing along with a leather pilot's cap that had an inch of wool lining.

I was so excited that I was going to see this hockey game for the first time in my life that I didn't look both ways before running out from between two parked cars. The car, which was not going very fast since the street was covered in snow, hit me and I rolled over the hood, over the roof, down off the trunk of the car, and landed on the street. My brother saw the whole thing. I woke up in the Royal Victoria Hospital three days later in the middle of the night on a ward with about twelve other beds. Can you imagine what I felt as I called out to my mom in this strange place?

Later the next day, my parents and brother came to see me. They told me I had a brain concussion and a skull fracture. The doctor said that if I had not worn the pilot's cap I would have died. My brother Norm, who had ridden with me in the ambulance, told me that he could see the monitors in the ambulance and that I had been dead for about two minutes before they had revived me. As you know, after two minutes with no blood flow to the brain, the brain starts to deteriorate. I would have been retarded, but God had other plans for me.

Swimming on My Honeymoon

We honeymooned at the Wisconsin Dells, a vacation spot in central Wisconsin. One night, at about 11:30, I couldn't sleep so I told Sharon that I was going to go to the pool for a swim. Of course, at that time of night, the pool was closed and the pool area lights and the subsurface lights in the pool were turned off. I was not supposed to be there, but I decided to take a dip anyway.

During my swim, I got adventurous. I started to experiment with how long I could hold my breath under water. I was at the deep end and would hold my breath as long as possible and then buy some more time by slowly emptying my lungs as I counted off the seconds. When I absolutely had to have air, I would push off the bottom and rushed to the top. I did this for about 20 minutes.

Then, as I was getting better at this and trying to break my records, I tried it again. This time I was now out of breath and figured I'd float to the top naturally. But I was wrong. Without air you don't rise as fast as with lungs that are full. I needed air so I pushed my legs down to reach for the floor and realized I was nowhere near the floor. I was suspended half way between the surface and the bottom and couldn't push off of anything. Remember, there were no lights to tell me where the surface was, so I didn't know which way was up. I realized I was going to drown so I stopped moving my arms to swim and laid limp in the water. Just as the moment came when I would have had to take a breath, my head ever so gently broke the surface of the water and I knew that the little bit of air in my body was enough to take me to the surface.

I then realized that I almost drowned on my honeymoon.

Heading For the Swamp

I started a sign painting business in Wilson. Of course, as is always the case, business drops off in the wintertime. People are either saving their money for Christmas or recovering from Christmas debt; they simply don't have money for signage.

So, one particular year, when business dwindled, I went to work for a concrete laying company. Unfortunately, there were days when it became so cold that even we couldn't work – the weather wasn't conducive to laying concrete. I remember getting up one day at 6:00 am to make a trip to Raleigh with the crew. When I got there, we were told that we were being sent home due to weather. About 8:00 pm that night I got a call from the contractor to ask me if I could take some pay checks to another crew that was working in Manteo on the coast. They couldn't work either. They were held up in a motel waiting for warmer weather. The boss said that since we couldn't work that day at least I could earn some money by delivering the paychecks to the crew in Manteo, which is on Roanoke Island on the other side of Pamlico Sound.

I left the house at about 9pm to make the four to five hour one-way trip. The temperature was about eighteen degrees with a wind chill factor of about ten. And to make matters worse, I battled sleep for about an hour in the final leg of my trip. I had fallen asleep several times only to shake myself awake for a little while longer. Just before reaching the bridge that goes over the Pamlico Sound, I rode the two mile stretch of raised road with swamp on both sides leading to the bridge. I hadn't seen another car in about forty-five minutes. It was about 12:30 am.

I finally fell asleep for the last time while traveling about sixty miles per hour. The last thing I remember seeing was that I was definitely in my lane. Then, I felt a solid jolt to my car and when I awoke I was heading for the ditch on the other side of the road. I had awakened just in time to regain control of my car and stopped with the front of my car just about to go down the snow covered embankment into the swamp. I backed up and went across the road and then saw the reverse lights of the car that had just grazed my left front bumper.

When we backed up alongside each other, we both rolled down or windows. The first thing he said was, "You fell asleep at the wheel didn't you?" I answered in the affirmative. He then said, "I'm Pastor so and so's son and we are having an all night prayer meeting at our church in Manteo. My father asked me to go home (on the main land) to get his Bible. I told him that I believe this whole thing was a divine appointment. He agreed.

What I realized through this was that angels preserved me that night and that there must be a divinely ordered plan for me. Many people experience these same things but just don't make the prophetic connection. I believe they think that way because they either simply don't believe they are that important to God or that there is no particular purpose for them being here on the planet. Our destinies are revealed to us over many years and if we don't pay attention to the little details, we'll miss it.

This is why I have learned to keep a journal and have decided – with the encouragement of my eldest son of course – to write my experiences in this book. The steps of the righteous are ordered.

Chapter Five

A Dream & Jane's Dying Mom

One morning, before waking, I had a dream wherein I saw an old woman, dressed in a cotton bath robe with purple and blue flowers and green stems. She came walking out of the darkness with a intravenous pole in her hand by her side. The pole had four to five IV bags hanging on it and she had them all stuck in different areas of her body. Some were even up her nose and in her mouth. She had silver hair and a boyish hair cut.

As I was looking at her I heard God say, "What do you see, Mike?" I answered, "I see a very sick woman." He said, "What are *you* going to do about it?" I said, "I don't know but *You* do." He then shouted at me and said, "Get it out of there!"

I began to pray fervently for this woman, binding the spirit of infirmity and loosing the spirit of life and health. I prayed a shotgun prayer saying the things I'd read about in lessons on prayer.

Then the dream ended.

When I awoke, around 7:00 am, I heard my wife talking on the phone in the kitchen just outside the bedroom. The door was cracked so I could hear what Sharon was saying. She was talking to a woman we knew named Jane who was asking Sharon to pray for her elderly mother who was in intensive care at Wilson Memorial Hospital. The doctors said she had only twenty-four hours to live, and unfortunately, they had said that the previous day.

After listening to the conversation for about three minutes I realized I had seen this woman in my dream. I got up, went into the kitchen and asked Sharon to ask Jane if her mother had short silver hair and a boyish hair cut. She said, "Yes!" Then I asked, "Does she have a bathrobe with purple and blue flowers and green stems on it?" She said, "Yes!" Finally, I asked, "Does she have all kinds of IV tubes in her?" She said, "Yes!" Immediately, without hesitation, I grabbed the phone and said, "Jane, I just had a dream about your mother. What is going on?" She told me all the details of the doctor's prognosis. I said, "Well Jane, in the dream God told me to pray for her and said, "Get it out of there!" I believe your mom's going to be alright." Jane thanked me and she told me that the whole family was going to the hospital as soon as visiting hours opened up at 9:00 am, which, at point in time, was going to be in two hours.

At about 9:15 am, we got a call from Jane saying that when they saw her mother, she was awake, out of the coma, without the IVs, sitting up in bed, talking.

About six months later, I was in church and Jane brought her mother over to me and said, "Mom, this is Mike Killion. He's the one who had the dream about you in the hospital and prayed for you." Then, her mother came closer to me, held my face in her hands and thanked me.

Notice, God didn't say, "Stand back! I'm going to heal

her!" Instead, he visited a man and commanded him to speak His plan. It says in Amos, "The Lord God will do nothing unless He first reveals His secrets unto His servants the prophets." Does God desire to share the finest details of His plans with us? Yes, of course, and if we are His friends, He will.

Sure, the Lord could do it all alone, without us, but He would rather do it with us and through us because we are His workmanship. This is a partnership, a team effort. We are His ambassadors.

Chapter Six

Boils & Healing

Years ago, in the mid-1970s, when we were still living in Milwaukee, Sharon and I received a phone call from a friend (I'll call him John) who was in the hospital with seven boils in his mouth. John was crying and he wanted us to come and pray for him. He was desperate. The doctor had told him there was nothing else that could be done and that there were no more antibiotics to administer.

John was a heavy smoker, but wanted everyone to think he had quit. Personally, I saw his bout with boils as retribution for his dishonesty and had little faith to believe God would heal him.

So, we (especially I) reluctantly went and prayed for him.

When we arrived and began to pray I began to think in my mind that John was getting what he deserved; he was an open sinner and it was his lot in life to suffer through this. My prayer went like this (Note: I've put my thoughts, that I had while I was praying, in parenthesis.).

"O, Lord, heal Jim (Fat chance!). He needs your healing touch right now (It ain't gonna happen any time soon). We ask that you heal him right now because he is your son (So what! He deserves to suffer). Send your healing to Jim (I know you're mad at him Lord. Give it to him Lord!). In the name of Jesus, amen

(We'll see!).

After praying, Sharon and I visited a while and then went home. The next morning we got a call from John at about 9:00 am and he was ecstatic saying, "Mike, I'm healed! The boils are gone! The doctor said I can go home! I'm packing my stuff! I'm coming home. Thank you for praying for me." I rejoiced with him and said goodbye. But, I was confused.

Today, I am still confused about healing and despite all the books that have been written about healing, it is still a mystery. And yet, as the story shows, we don't need to know a lot about healing or have a lot of experience in it or get all the words right or have the right attitude to be used by the Lord to heal others. And, believe it or not, we don't even have to be in agreement with God when He is determined to bless someone. John's faith expressed through his request for prayer was far more powerful than my inability to pray with the right spirit. The love of God was far more powerful in that moment than my misguided, half-hearted, and self-righteous attitude. God saw past my shallowness because He knew my heart was toward Him; so, He used me despite me, to show John and me that He will go to any length to make all things new.

Chapter Seven

The Faulty Plot Map

After I moved to Charlotte, my mother died and I used my inheritance to build a house. With about three weeks of construction left to go, I was really excited about moving in.

Then I had this dream one morning.

In the dream, I got a phone call from the builder who said, "Mr. Killion, we were putting together your closing package and found another plot map at the courthouse and it shows a different lot-line on your property. It shows that you didn't buy a rectangular plot but a trapezoid, and the lot-line goes through your kitchen. We're going to have to stop building until you can locate your neighbor and buy that small triangular piece of his land. When you have the deed in hand, fax it to us, and we'll resume building."

The Lord then proceeded to show me what I had to do to fix this situation: While still in the dream, I got off the phone with the builder and then got on the phone with my real estate attorney. After I explained to the attorney everything I was told by the builder's call, the attorney said to me, "What do you want me to do about this, Mike?" I said, "I want you to write the builder an official letter on your letterhead and tell him that he is responsible for the mistake; that he decided where to place the house; that he missed the other plot map at the courthouse; and that the patient doesn't tell the surgeon where to slice him up." The attorney agreed and within a week the builder had found my neighbor (who was, at that time, living in Virginia), purchased the land, and called me back saying they had purchased the additional land for $4000.00 and was sending me the deed and would resume building the next day.

When I woke up, the whole dream played out in real life. Within moments if waking up, the builder called me and said everything I was told by the builder in my dream. And, when I hung-up with the builder, I knew how to handle the situation. In the end, I was given the deed to an additional slice of land, just as I was shown in my dream.

Through that dream God was showing me, "*You are not to have one iota of apprehension over this problem, for through this I am extending your tent pegs.*" Father was teaching me directly in His school of the Holy Spirit that He wants to share His plans with us, even down to the finest detail. However, everyone has this potential but not everyone is listening; nor are they setting themselves in a position to hear.

Chapter Eight

Reign Over the Rain

In the seventies, after answering the call to ministry, my wife, Sharon, and I felt we were to move from Milwaukee, Wisconsin to Springfield, Missouri to attend Bible school. We had just bought a townhouse in northwest Milwaukee, so it meant we would have to sell the house in order to move. Months before, I felt I had heard the Lord say to me, "Streamline your operation and be ready to move within forty-eight hours." So we paid up our bills, cancelled some insurance, and began to gather boxes for packing.

Selling the townhouse would be tricky since we lived in a complex next to a Hindu family with wild children. These children would play just outside our door and mark up the siding by drawing pictures with colored chalk. The young son was once seen standing on a car roof urinating down onto the pavement. I thought our place would never sell if buyers saw this when looking at our place. But God had a plan.

One day Sharon met a lady at the bank, who said she was a realtor. Of course, in the course of their conversation, Sharon told her we were interested in selling our townhouse but that we had troublesome neighbors. The lady then boldly said she could sell the place within ten days. We jumped at the offer and signed the contract. In ten days the place was sold. For us, it was a miracle! And yet there was more to come.

On the day of the move, we loaded the U-Haul truck with the help of another couple. We were promised by another couple that they would help us as well, but they said they would be late due to a previous obligation. Nevertheless, Sharon and I, along with the other couple, began packing the truck when all of a sudden dark clouds moved in over us. Immediately, we were motivated to work even faster, before the deluge hit. Amazingly, when the rain began pouring, it seemed the clouds were dropping their water all at once onto our neighborhood, and yet we were surprised that no rain was hitting our townhouse. In fact, there was no rain within fifty feet of our front door. When the other two arrived, they told us that they drove through the storm and could hardly see beyond a few feet in front of their car on their way over from across town. They also said that when they drove up to our place it was like driving into the eye of the storm.

We continued to pack the truck and as we were loading the last piece, the heavy rains showed up. I shut the door of the truck and ran inside. We had been asking the Lord to hold back the rain and we all knew that God had answered our prayer long enough for us to finish the job.

As I look back at this event, it is obvious that this was the first of other occurrences where my prayers for weather adjustments were answered.

Chapter Nine

Experiencing His Promises

Years ago, when I was living in Elm City, North Carolina, there had been several tornados that came into the area where we were living. On one occasion, we could look out our bay window, over the farmer's fields, and see them coming our way.

On one occasion, we saw a tornado headed toward a wooded area on the west side of our house. We knew it was coming our way and yet when it entered the woods, it disappeared – or so we thought. The next thing we knew is that the tornado set down again on the other side of our house and continued east.

My wife and I looked at each other and wondered if we were protected, again, as we were in northwest Milwaukee. That was our only conclusion. We had just seen the direct intervention of God on our behalf, up close and personal, and it was far more impactful than any act of providence we could have heard from someone else or read in a book.

Now, why did I tell you that story? Well, people who have *not* been thoroughly tested have a shallow testimony; when someone asks them if they've experienced God's power, first-hand, they oftentimes can only quote a maxim or recite someone else's experience. It doesn't carry a lot of power. God puts us through tests so that when we pass them, we will be a stronger, more effective conduit in the hand of God for those who are in need. It is those hardships which try our metal and give power to our words, which, when spoken, move the heavens and the earth.

Selah (Pause and think on these things).

Chapter Ten

The King & I

In the late 1970s, after spending some time in a conservative fundamentalist church, the Lord began to reveal to Sharon and I that there was more to His Spirit than what we were experiencing. We learned that what we needed was the baptism of the Holy Spirit, which led us to attend a more charismatic church down the road. After a few months, I received my first prophetic word of destiny. Pastor Sam Peterson picked me out of the crowd and said that I was supposed to study the life of King David because his life was to be a pattern for my life. He also said that if I became acquainted with David's life I would better understand the events I would experience in my journey with the Lord and would be able to receive what God had for me.

Of course, this excited me because, at that time, all I had was an elementary concept of David's life. Pastor Peterson's word filled me with great anticipation of the revelation soon to come regarding my purpose. Yet, as I became aware of the process David underwent in his life in order to fulfill his prophetic destiny, I was shaken. And now, as I look back on my life, I can see that my processing has been much like David's.

David's road:

1. He was picked out from amongst his brothers to receive a

great destiny as a leader even though he was the least of his brethren.

2. Once he was "christened" he was sent back to obscurity. Then He was called out of obscurity into the forefront to complete a task, like playing the harp and singing songs to Saul to soothe the savage beast. Then he was sent back to his menial job – tending sheep. You would think that if you received a charge calling you to do an important job in the future that you would start preparing for it and be tutored by the best mentors. Just as the sons of kings who are called to take over their father's throne one day, the young ones are separated from the rank-and-file to be given the best of education and tutoring because in regular schools they don't teach what kings have to learn to do their jobs.

Nevertheless, David spent time in the military and that was a very important part of his preparation. He learned about protecting the nation and the rise and fall of nations. I never spent time in the military but I have spent a lot of time studying history and the rise and fall of nations. This is all about training for reigning.

As David began to show great skill and promise as a leader, it aroused the spirits of jealousy and competition in the one he was serving, King Saul. I have experienced this too, for as God began to show Himself through me I would find that my pastors would exhibit spirits of competition, manipulation, and control. I learned about submitting to authority and would often hear that "Your gifts will make room for you. You didn't have to push yourself to the forefront." But that only works if you are serving a leader who is secure in his own gifts and is a releaser, not a controller. Therefore, like David who was driven out of Saul's house and into exile, I too have been removed from several churches who told me various things like, "This church is not ready for you yet" or "You're too far out there for people to understand."

So, like David, I have spent decades on the road, searching for acceptance by a leader who is a true father who wants more for his sons than he wants for himself. So far I can name three like this and I am proud to name them.

- Bill Britton, of Springfield, Missouri, my first real father. I worked in his ministry as the manager of his Overcomer Correspondence School. I played golf with him and ate lunch with him many times. He spent time with me and listened when I wanted to share a new insight. He also corrected me in a way that made me want to change. Where are these guys today?

- Tim Miller, of Rocky Mount, North Carolina, was my pastor, but he was a young man himself coming up. He learned from me and I lead him to a new level of revelation in the Word. When he ate it up and ministered in the new light, it split his church down the middle because there were people in his church who were of the old order and didn't want to move up. Tim accepted me and befriended me and gave me standing. He allowed me to preach on the Tabernacle of Moses for five to six Wednesday nights. He turned his pulpit over to me and that displayed trust and acceptance.

- Mark DeVito, of Pineville, North Carolina, who runs an "open church" and doesn't give his sermon until those in the pew who have something from the Lord have had a chance to give out what they have received from the Lord. Mark made it possible for me to go to Peru four times.

There were others who accepted me and brought me out of obscurity but they were young and I was more of a teacher to them but they were in the pastor's chair. Benny Humphries, missionary to Tarapoto, Peru, was my roommate at Morningstar School Of Ministry, and I have ministered in his church in Peru on four occasions. Thanks Ben.

Back to David's road:

3. David was mocked by someone very close to him. That's been my lot too. When someone close to you mocks your calling and abilities I have found that even this is a test. Can you be talked out of it? Can you, like Jeremiah, "be not afraid of their faces"? What will you trust? Who did Job listen to? Did Job stave off the critics?

4. David lost his wife. So did I. David had other wives. I haven't.

Chapter Eleven

Time Warps

Remember Joshua's long day that allowed him more time to defeat the enemy? If you are ascending the hill of the Lord, which I refer to as hedging into the Holy of Holies, where the greatest supernatural element exists, you will experience manipulations of space, matter, and time just like Jesus, Joshua, and Moses.

In John 17 we see what I call "The Great Exchange" chapter. This is where Jesus said, "Father, what you have give me, I gave to them. You are in me and I am in them and they are in me and I am in you." This is profound! We are *in* God! In Him, there is no sin, sickness, death, or limitation. Our only limitation is that we are nothing except what we are in Him and we "can do nothing lest the Father shows us first."

When I studied the tabernacle of Moses and taught it at Tim Miller's church for those five to six Wednesday nights, I began to experience warps of time and circumstances. Many call these miracles. I can agree to that.

There was a time when Jesus was in His glorified body that He could walk on the floor and walk through a wall. He submitted to the laws of matter so that the floor could support Him but also caused the laws of matter to submit to Him so He could walk through the wall. He had full mastery of scientific laws. If we are in Him and He is in us, then what is true for Him is true for us. Paul said we "know in part and prophesy (speak) in part, but when that which is perfect is come, then the part shall be done away."

People, faithful ones, those of you who have not drunk the cool-aid and swallowed the "strong delusions" of our time understand that we are in the last days. We are in the Third Day from Jesus; He is healing us (Hosea 6:1-2). He is curing us of our part-realm thinking. This is the day when "all things that are hidden shall be revealed." We are coming to the time of the full outpouring of His Spirit. Dispensations O-V-E-R-L-A-P. There is always a "first fruits crop" of barley or "early ripeners." We should be seeing these things more and more.

My Time Warp Experience

In the 90's when I was studying the Tabernacle in detail over the course of many weeks, I would sit down to study about 9:00 pm and get lost in the anointing. I would often feel alone in a bubble. I would study through the night and be brought back to reality because I heard my wife open the back door as she returned home from work on third shift. I had been "away" in study. Eight or nine hours seemed like two or three hours. I had been raptured in a time warp. In the natural world, time had continued as normal, but as far as I was concerned, hours were minutes.

Expect this to happen more and more. Expect amazing things.

Chapter Twelve

A Problem on the Job

I used to be in the sign painting business. On one occasion, I had painted a four foot by eight foot plywood sign for a business and had to deliver it and hang it with bolts in the four corners on their metal building. Even before I left home I knew I had a problem: How was I going to tighten the bolts? Normally, you have to put a wrench on the nut while you tighten the bolt. You need two wrenches and you have to hold the nut while tightening the bolt. This sign had to be hung eighteen feet high on the wall. I was stuck.

I had asked God for wisdom earlier that morning on how I could do this. Once I got up there I was successful in drilling the holes and inserting the hex head bolts through the face of the sign. With that done, the sign hung with bolts in from the front and now it was time to put the nuts on the bolts on the inside of the building. So, I took my ladder to the inside of the building and screwed the nuts on and tightened them as much as I could by hand. The problem is, you typically need two wrenches – one on the nut to hold it in place and one on the bolt head to tighten the screw into the bolt. I could not be on both sides at the same time.

The employees all came out to see the sign being hung.

They wondered how I would tighten the bolts. I wondered too. Actually, I wasn't wondering; I was praying. I ascended the ladder not knowing what to do. When I got there I heard a voice say, "Just start turning the bolts." I did. As I turned the wrench, the bolts started to tighten! No one was on the inside holding the nuts from turning with the bolts. I just turned the wrench by faith and they tightened. I descended the ladder and said to the owner, "There's your new sign." He said he and the guys were wondering how I'd get those bolts to tighten. I said, "Angels!"

It ended up that God and His angels made me look like a genius.

Chapter Thirteen

The Hurricane Splits

When Sharon and I were in Missouri and we were seeking the Lord about moving to Wilson, North Carolina, we were seeking God for clear direction, for signs pointing the way. One day Hurricane David blew up from the south and was heading for North Carolina. We watched its track on the national radar on television. It was national news. We wondered if we were watching a sign that would point the way.

When David reached the North Carolina border, it fizzled out. We looked at each other and said something like, "Hmmm."

Not long after that another hurricane arose. I forgot what they named it. This one came from out in the Atlantic, east of North Carolina, headed for the Outer Banks. As it came up to the coast of North Carolina, it split into two. Then, one half went up into Virginia and the other half went down into South Carolina.

We turned to each other and said, "There's something about North Carolina!" This observation was a very big part of our decision to move to North Carolina. We had been lead here by a prophet. Nature was being used to confirm the way. Our steps were being ordered in this move.

Chapter Fourteen

The Dark Night

Nobody likes them! People who are not having this experience or never have cannot know what it is and will reject those who tout it as a true experience in the life of the believer. The "dark night" experience can be explained as the time when God seems to withdraw the Holy Spirit from you and He just lets you sit there with no spirit or motivation to do anything, including getting out of bed in the morning.

The best way I can show this is when you look at the life of Jesus. Jesus is our pattern. If you're serious about being like Jesus and walking in His ways, you will go through the process He endured. You must take up your cross and follow Him daily. Since I had asked for Him to shine through me early in my Christian experience, I had to "walk the walk that Jesus walked." I didn't realize what I had signed up for. They didn't tell me I'd have to "die!" You see, you have to die first so He can bring you back to life anew with power. It's not a physical death. What you have to die to is your agenda, your wrong thinking, and your self-centeredness. Since we can't do this to ourselves, because we want to "live for Christ," He has to impose this death upon our soul, which is our mind (what we think), our will (what we want), and our emotions (what we feel). And this death must happen because what we think, what we want, and what we feel is often contrary to what the Lord thinks, wants, and feels.

When He withdraws His power from you, you are back to operating on the self-spirit (soul) power you had before you encountered the Holy Spirit. Your prayers seem to go nowhere and you think He has left you. But the truth is that He is the Surgeon hovering over you through this whole thing while you are under spiritual anesthesia. You could also call this the "winepress of God" because when you get squeezed the everything inside you comes out. And through this time you're desperate for a touch from Him because you think He isn't there. But God is checking to see what you'll do under this pressure. It's a type of the Great Tribulation to come and, as always happens in tribulation, many "fall away" when the heat gets too hot, which explains why few ever make it past the initial stages of the Dark Night. In a Dark Night of the soul, you are actually going through your own personal tribulation as a practice run so you can, among other things, counsel people as they walk through their own great tribulation.

As for me, I actually went through two dark nights – the first was for about seven years and the second was for about three years. And I didn't do too well.

The first time I backslid from the Lord; as a result, His hand of discipline left me for a season. I felt like God had left me. I felt all alone. At one time I got so despondent I cursed at God and told Him to go jump in the lake or take me home. Yes, I wanted to die! I didn't care. My skin would often feel like it was crawling because my understanding and agendas were dying before my eyes. As far as I was concerned, I was a walking corpse. I wanted to escape this hell I was in. I thought I could sin the unpardonable sin by cussing at Him using the "F" word. And you know what He did? Absolutely nothing! He just let me sit there and wallow. I felt like Jesus on the Cross who thought the Father had forsaken Him, when, in reality, the Father never actually left but was in Him reconciling the world to Himself.

Yet, through various circumstances, I was reminded of my Father's love and favor toward me, which, according to my perception at that time, restored our connection. I realized then by experience that I can do nothing without the Holy Spirit. The reality of leaning the entirety of one's self upon Him can't just be a concept you read about. Your dependence on Him must be worked deeply into you.

As I said, I didn't pass the test. He returned His Spirit to me and I thought I had passed but I hadn't. I had to go around that mountain again several years later.

After a few years, I experienced a series of disappointments and I got disillusioned again. This was the beginning of the second "dark night"; in hindsight, it came gradually and I didn't recognize it, but it lasted about three years. I became totally self-absorbed looking for consolation and satisfaction. This time my "hissy-fit" – my response to the disappointments – cost me my wife. She told me, "You need to move out and seek God to find out what you should be when you grow up." I had told her that it would take one and a half years to complete Paralegal School and now we were two and a half years into it and I was unable to pass the accounting course so it looked like I would never complete the degree. I was working at a local food store part time, barely earning enough money to pay for my lunches at school. She was supporting the family and as the children were coming to the end of High School she knew our expenses were going to increase.

So, when Sharon told me to "move out," I left and I moved in with a fellow student in Paralegal school. She and her son lived nearby in a one bedroom apartment. Her boyfriend had moved out as I moved in. He called Sharon and told her that I was having an affair with his girlfriend. Sharon didn't believe it until she came to visit and asked some pointed questions. Ultimately, my marriage was lost to bad choices.

However, that is not the end of the story. Accompanying the negative story is the account of how from rock bottom, a way to the next phase of development ensued. After I lost my way of life, I had plenty of time to think. The wave on the beach had receded and the next wave was scheduled to come soon. I had to make a new life for myself. God then began to put me back together through some interventions. As painful as the transition from a "happy" and "secure" home was, I felt that the Holy Spirit was doing His part as the Paraclete (the One Who comes alongside us) and coming alongside me to see me through this paradigm shift.

I landed a good enough job to allow me to qualify for a loan on a mobile home. Soon, I was working and living independently. In this, I achieved a certain degree of security and I could seek God for the next step down the road to a new life. My eldest son, Joel had graduated from high school and enrolled in Morningstar University in Charlotte, North Carolina. The next year, at his encouragement, I moved to Charlotte to enter the school as a first year student while he was in his second year.

After my first year of study I was hired as a teacher at Charlotte Christian School where my yearly contract was for the most money and benefits than I had ever made in my life. The people I met there were also an added bonus; I met some wonderful Christian educators who became my friends. I felt the blessings of God had started to come upon me.

Within thirty days of arriving in Charlotte, my mother died and I received my inheritance and with it I built a house and paid it off so as not to have a mortgage. With these blessings I felt as though the heavy hand of training and discipline I knew while in my dark night of the soul had subsided. As I look back over the last eleven years here in Charlotte, where I now live, I have not had another Dark Night experience, and I believe that that is an indication that I had successfully graduated to a new level of understanding and deliverance from self-centeredness.

Since coming to Charlotte and fellowshipping with many people on the prophetic level, I now have a better sense of who I am, what I have as spiritual gifts, and what I'm supposed to be doing. Now it is 2012 and I am experiencing the greatest level of joy, peace, patience, and fulfillment than I've ever know before.

By bringing us through the Dark Night, the Lord is testing our faithfulness to see if we will leave Him like the disciples did when He went to Calvary and they thought the dream had died. My dreams had died or so I thought. However, that was the kicker; they were *my* dreams. God used the dark night to burn selfish ambition out of me. God let me stew until I stewed myself out. He wouldn't give me a place to rest and He wouldn't kill me like I wanted Him to. So, after three to four years I decided it was time to return to Him. You see, if your hand is in the hand of the man who stills the waters, your major life events are all a set up, because, despite us and our choices, "…all things work together and are [fitting into a plan] for good to and for those who love God and are called according to [His] design and purpose" (Romans 8:28, Amplified). This is why I no longer see the Dark Night as dark. Instead, I see it as a blessing. Therefore, when disappointments rise up, there is no thought of turning back. I know my steps are ordered. Now, I have such a strong inward constitution that I can walk through the Valley of the Shadow of Death and fear nothing.

And this is an assurance we must all have as we enter the Day of Jacob's Trouble. What God is raising up in this day is a people who will stand like a strong tower in a dark world. We are coming into a time of darkness where the masses will be searching for someone to grab onto who has the clarity and the strength that I am now able to exhibit even though the world is getting darker around me every moment.

Chapter Fifteen

"This Place Is Coming Down"

When my sons were young, Sharon and I had purchased a lifetime membership to PTL in Fort Mill, South Carolina, which included, among other things, camping privileges. During one particular year we went camping with our Starcraft pop-up camper. As the vacation came to a close and we were driving out of the campground, we drove past the south side of the Grand Hotel. At that moment I heard a voice in my head say, "This place is coming down; it's built on a false foundation."

Well, we all know the rest of the story. In the ensuing years, PTL came down and the ministry and buildings fell into ruins.

These were the days when God was developing the prophetic anointing in me. At this time when I knew that every word from God had to be tested, I had no confirmation that it was true. It took fulfillment to confirm and years later I received that confirmation.

Sometime later as I began to realize this gift was maturing in me, a friend of ours spoke to us about her daily habit of journaling. This drove me to start keeping a journal of my own so I could see and keep a history of how God was truly speaking to me. Many people are being developed in the prophetic and don't even know it. They receive a real word from the Lord and dismiss it as their own thought or feeling. But, Romans 12:2 says "Do not be conformed to this world (this age), [fashioned after and adapted to its external, superficial customs], but be transformed (changed) by the [entire] renewal of your mind [by its new ideals and its new attitude], so that you may prove [for yourselves] what is the good and acceptable and perfect will of God, even the thing which is good and acceptable and perfect [in His sight for you]" (Amplified). In other words, as our mind is transformed by the Word over time, our mind (soul) is exchanged for His to such a degree that what we receive on the wavelength of our own thoughts is actually His thoughts.

Chapter Sixteen

What to Study

God gets specific with the way He trains you. With me, He even directed me on things to study. At times, He would even cause certain books, tapes, and newsletters to find their way into my hands. He also gave me my thirsts; thirst for knowledge and thirst for certain subjects.

As I look back over the last thirty-five years I see that my educational development in the Word has followed a specific trail. It shows that we all have certain gifts and we are not called to know it all. Instead, we are called to specialize in various truths and purposes This is the day of the specialist. My specialties are:

1. End time prophecy
2. Religious and secular history that illuminates Biblical prophecy
3. Our walk in the spirit and becoming what He has destined us to become; this includes the pits we all fall into by His hand. (e.g. Joseph, Daniel, and Paul.)
4. The true identity of Israel and the "strong delusions" surrounding it.
5. Conspiracy theories and the rise and fall of nations. Here is a short list of some of the subjects God spoke to

me to study and write about through mind to mind communication:

1. "Study the things that happened at midnight for it shows what will happen at the time of the change and the order that I will do it in."

2. "Study the remnant!" (This lengthy study included the words, "afflicted, scattered, and regathered," and led me into my study on true Israel.)

3. "Study the Lost Sheep of the house of Israel."

4. "Study the words, "hide, hid, hidden, hiding," and the word, "until." (This study led me to write my articles called, "The Hidden Ones" and "The Place of Immunity."

5. "Look at the days of Noah more closely; what are preachers not seeing?" (This study led me to write the article, "Times of Silence," and why God seems to take His messengers off the scene and hide them away for their protection. It also illustrates that the Lord closes the door on rebellious ones.

6. "Is it enough to simply believe in your heart and confess with your mouth that Jesus Christ is Lord in order to be saved?"

In time, I saw that it was not enough to just believe and confess because I realized that even the devil does that. He knows who Jesus is. He knows Jesus is God's Son and holds that lofty position and that's what Satan hates and opposes. Many people do the same. Knowing, believing, and confessing is not enough.

All God's enemies do this but because there has not been a heart transplant or conversion in the inner man, they are still sitting on the throne of their own lives, calling their own shots.

Someone I know tells the story of how she watched Billy Graham for ten years reciting the sinner's prayer every time she watched him and nothing happened. There was no notable change. No power to change. Then, one day she was reading a book where the sinner's prayer appeared at the back of the book and she prayed the prayer. The next day she says she woke up and knew she was different because something happened inside that caused her to see and feel differently.

I have the same testimony. One night I finished reading Hal Lindsey's "Late Great Planet Earth" and prayed the sinner's prayer at the end of the book. The next day at the breakfast table I knew things were different. I felt a new way of seeing the world had come to me. I felt like I was on another planet living life according to a new set of rules and that I was now a "wanderer and sojourner in a strange land."

You can believe and confess all you want but without a heart, mind, and eye transplant, and the power that comes with that new way, you're just a religious degenerate putting on a show. There is a religious demon on the loose that makes people believe they are "saved" when they are not. This false conversion can ensnare people in a false sense of acceptance for their whole lives and when the going gets tough we see what happens. They bolt from the fold. Paul speaks in Second Thessalonians chapter two of a "strong delusion" and false conversions are one of those strong delusions.

In the soon coming Great tribulation we will see many "Christians" wash out because they were led to believe that easy-believism – simply believing and speaking – was enough. Many have been "converted" this way and have never learned to "present their bodies a living sacrifice," wholly submitted to Father's discipline and training.

One of the purposes of the Great Tribulation is to separate the sheep from the goats, the wheat from the tares, and the good figs from the bad figs. When the ten plagues came upon on Egypt, the first four fell on Israel as well, but after that, a difference was made between the two nations. I believe that happened in order to make God's own people serious, to cut the shenanigans, and to get their minds right. Once He proves Himself to His own people, then He will judge the nations.

Chapter Seventeen

Jack-in-the-Box

First Corinthians speaks of the coming time of the change. In the Book of Revelation, John was told to "come up hither." God wants to call all of us higher into Himself and turn us into another people.

Back when I was studying the tabernacle and experiencing those time warps, I had a vision where I was a Jack in the Box and God was slowly turning the crank, tightening the spring, bringing me closer and close to a release from "the box."

Immediately, I began to think and that was my greatest mistake. I began to think about what would happen if I continued to study and worship as I was doing. I began to imagine what it would be like if I continued in that place of commitment to being with Him and the box popped open. What would happen? What would it be like? What was waiting on the other side of the release? How would I live if I ascended into the higher realms? Would I stay there? Would I come down to "reality" and continue on living in the lower realms? What would life be like? Would I be able to relate to my family and friends like "normal?" Would I live in a spaced-out, catatonic state forever or would God allow me to have a "normal" life with my wife and kids? I was full of questions. I feared the unknown.

Soon, the fear took over and I backed off. I folded up my books and notes and set them aside in F.E.A.R., which is "False Evidence Appearing Real." I avoided getting back into that state of consecration because I didn't know what would happen. It makes my heart flutter in apprehension just to speak of it now. Sometime later, God sent me into my experience with the Dark Night of the soul where He seemed to withdraw from me for seven years. During those seven years my energy was sapped and it was a struggle to get the energy to go about my daily life. Cutting the grass was a chore and I had to force myself to do it. Depression set in. I sat around a lot and ate indiscriminately and ballooned to 218 pounds. Life was tasteless. In my mind I had no reason to live except to be with my wife and kids. They made life bearable. God was bringing me low. He was killing me.

Many people are now looking for a "happy" life - whatever that is. They are looking for a peaceful life where certain things can be relied on. Most people are acting as if they don't know what day they are living in or that we are in a war. The Day of Jacob's Trouble will be here soon and may even be here now. God is taking many people who have made a commitment to live for Jesus and be His servant and is taking them to Boot Camp. But they forget the commitment they have made and when the survival training comes they get disillusioned and fall away. But, that's the whole purpose of our tribulation before the Great Tribulation.

Now, I'm sixty-four and single and asking Him to crank

the crank again and bring me to the breaking point. I'm telling him that this time I will not run!

Chapter Eighteen

Threatened With a Knife

In the Old Testament God told disobedient and idolatrous Israel that He would scatter them among the Gentiles and draw out a sword after them. God was going to make life hard for them for two reasons:

- As punishment for their sins, and
- As training for reigning.

I don't know why we as human beings can't take God at His word, be obedient, and advance without trouble but that's the way it seems to be. I'm sure many military recruits wish they could just become lean-mean-fighting-machines without the harsh training and survival exercises.

I am reminded of Moses' forty years as a shepherd in the house of Jethro, sitting on his education, after being raised up in Egypt. I remember Joseph "wasting" away in an Egyptian prison after telling his brothers of his high calling. I remember David having to run for his life after being threatened by his father-in-law who was jealous of his popular. Then there was Paul on the back side of the Arabian Desert being cleansed for fourteen years and learning a new way of thinking after his conversion.

Why is down the way up?

Back in the late nineties after I had moved to Charlotte, I took a job with Bi-Lo Supermarket as a meat clerk. I was hired by a very nice man who was the manager of the department and he seemed to know the Lord. After about four months, a new assistant manager came on board. He was not nice! He didn't know the Lord.

The relationships between all of my co-workers were great. We often shared wonderful conversation as we worked or as we fellowshipped over lunch. A great sense of commitment and cohesion developed over time. Throughout my time there, I gradually began to share that I was a Christian and had experienced some miracles in my life. That was very encouraging to most of them. However, my testimony rubbed the new assistant manager the wrong way.

Gradually over the course of several weeks he began to get belligerent, critical, and down-right nasty toward me when I spoke. On many occasions he snapped at me with the intention of shutting me up, but I felt I was there to be an encouragement to the team. That's what I do. I am a missionary!

After this went on for some time the new assistant manager stood at his cutting table across the room and turned towards me and raising his fillet knife pointing it at me said, "If you don't shut up, I will kill you." He then turned back to face his work. The manager then tried to change the conversation so as to diffuse a potentially flammable situation. Shortly, after further conversation the assistant said something nasty about me behind my back. Then he made another nasty statement about my testimony directly at me. I answered back defending my testimony and the assistant picked up his large butcher knife, walked over to within two feet of me, raised his knife to within 18 inches of my throat and said in a loud, forceful and irritated voice, "I told you; if you don't shut up right now, I will kill you!" I then looked at the department manager, which caused the assistant manager to drop his head. How's that for leadership?

At that point, I took off my apron and headed for the office to speak to the top manager of the store. I said to him that the assistant manager had committed three tort crimes against me (a) communicating a threat, (b) with a deadly weapon, and (c) intentional infliction of emotional distress - I really felt my life was threatened because of his tone of voice and anger. I asked for something to be done. The store manager said nothing and told me to return to my department and get back to work.

That is when I heard the Lord say, "Get out of here; they aren't going to do anything about it." So I left and drove home, jobless.

When I got home I saw there was a message on my answering machine. It was from Dr. Otto, principal of Charlotte Christian School, asking me to call him about the application I had filed for a teacher's assistant six months earlier when I was contemplating returning to teaching. Immediately, I called him back and left him a message to let him know I was still interested.

The next morning was Saturday and I arose early to paint the walls in the new house I had just built and moved in to. Dr. Otto called me and asked if I could come to an interview. I said

"When?" He said, "Now." I told him I was smack dab in the middle of painting and was all sweaty and covered in paint. He said, "No matter, come as you are." So I dropped everything and drove over to the school, with my earring in my ear. "Oh, great," I thought. "What a way to go to the interview of a lifetime. This man wants to see what I'm really like, in my natural state." I thought, "Okay, the earring stays in."

When I got into the interview, I told him I had been contemplating returning to teaching but had not been in a classroom for over ten years and had trashed my lesson plans. I thought serving a year as an assistant would help me transition to readiness for teaching. Dr. Otto then said, "Oh, I'm not interviewing you for an assistant's job. I want you as a teacher!" I dropped my jaw and after catching my breath I told him again that I didn't have any lesson plans and would have to start all over gathering a new file of plans. That's when he reached into a drawer and pulled out three thick binders of lesson plans, one for each level I would be assigned to. He then told me that the Art department head would be assigned to me as a mentor and would help me in every way I needed. He had just kicked out any excuse I could throw out as reasons why I couldn't do the job. He hired me on one condition: ditch the ear ring. Of course, I did and had a wonderful time teaching at Charlotte Christian School where I met many great servants of the Lord.

In short, I went from having my life threatened on a job for sharing my faith to a haven for God's servants within two days. My faith was restored and my fear was gone because I knew my steps were ordered.

Chapter Nineteen

Can You Hit God's Knuckleball?

God often speaks in parables. It makes us dig. It makes us think. It makes us *"hunger and thirst for righteousness."* Jesus often spoke in parables to the masses and then explained His words to His inner circle when He was alone with them. This was one way of determining who was serious about learning of Him and who would follow at all costs. Would they pay the price by deeply enquiring into the hidden meanings? God is not as interested in the quantity of people following Him as He is in the quality of their life in Him. The real test comes when the going gets tough. It's funny how people appreciate things more when they have to work for it.

This is a commentary on many churches today who are "seeker friendly" or "seeker sensitive." Seeker friendly churches make following Jesus easy implying you only have to do a minimum to be accepted. That wasn't so when Jesus was training His disciples. You remember when He told His disciples, "…If anyone desires to be My disciple, let him deny himself [disregard, lose sight of, and forget himself and his own interests] and take up his cross and follow Me [cleave steadfastly to Me, conform wholly to My example in living and, if need be, in dying, also]" (Matthew 16:24, Amplified).

One day He spoke to me the following, "Can you hit my

knuckleball?" God was speaking to me in an allegory. He was using a knuckleball pitcher to symbolize Himself delivering up knuckleballs to His people in this hour. I played baseball when I was a kid. I was a catcher. I know all about knuckleball pitches because we had a knuckleballer on our team at South Milwaukee High School.

Follow me on this line of thinking. It illustrates how God speaks to His people:

When I was young and didn't know Him – that is, when I was not born again and didn't even know anything about Him – He threw me slow balls, meaning He pitched thoughts and leadings to me slowly so I could ponder them and make decisions based on simple truths. From this I understood and accepted what He was saying because I was being dealt with on a simple level. This brought me to regeneration by His Spirit where my spiritual life in Him began.

After years as a newborn in Christ, He began to pitch me on deeper truths I call fastballs. Fastballs are harder to hit, but because they are straightforward truths, you can train yourself to hit them by judging their speed. Simple.

Then came God's curveball. Have you ever heard someone say, "They threw me a curve ball?" That means truth came to them but not as expected. The statement that was made was veiled in some mystery or riddle.

The ball leaves the pitcher's hands at one angle and takes a turn before it arrives at home plate. It requires more skill to hit.

Likewise, God will throw us curveballs when we are more mature to take us deeper so we will dig into truths more seriously. He is also, again, trying to determine who is serious about going all the way with Him. Who is able to discern truth from fiction in these days and the days ahead when God Himself will send us a "strong delusion" to carry away those who aren't serious? (See II Thessalonians 2) The current flood of lies and deception and our discernment of them will determine whether we are the wheat or the tares that must be separated in the coming judgments.

The knuckleball is another animal altogether. It is the hardest pitch to hit and the hardest truth to comprehend. It is the deepest parable to understand. In order to throw an actual knuckleball, the pitcher (who is the Lord in the metaphor) holds the ball differently, not in His fingers but with his fingertips and fingernails. When released, the ball (the Truth) does not follow a logical path that can be followed. The ball, instead, darts in different directions several times before it gets to the plate like a feather falling to the ground. These pitches (nuggets of truth) are hard to figure out. You don't know where the ball (train of God's thought) is going to end up. So it is with God's prophetic word today, when discerning what God will do in situations. This is why we must stay close to Him and constantly talk with Him. Ask for directions daily or even moment by moment. This is what is going to be necessary in the flood of lies that are coming upon the earth.

The knuckleball is so unpredictable that the catchers (another symbol of the believer) will often use a larger mitt to catch the throw. This speaks of our openness and diligence in searching out His message to us.

God has truth for all seekers but cannot share the deeper things with the careless. What He is putting us through is like Navy Seal training. Remember the movie *G.I. Jane*? The drill instructor would often ask the recruits for their resignation by asking them if they had come to the limit of their training.

God is doing this to us to see if we can go the distance. Many will fall away because they were "led to the Lord" by a preacher that told them that following Jesus would end all their troubles. No, when we walked in the world according to our own dictates, we were just trying to avoid hardship to make our lives easier. This is not what Jesus said we would experience. He told us we would walk against the grain and, as a result, suffer persecutions. The way of the world is easy but to walk in the kingdom cuts across everything the world says.

Jesus said that he who loves this life will lose it, but he who hates (rejects, walks away from, discards, etc.) it, will gain the kingdom.

Today, God is seeking those who will not run when the stuff hits the fan.

Chapter Twenty

No Super Bowl for the Panthers

The year after the Carolina Panthers lost the Super Bowl in XXXVIII, I was settling down in front of the television to watch the home opener for the next season. It was a Monday night and we were playing the Green Bay Packers who are my favorite team since I am from Wisconsin. Just before the kickoff I heard the Holy Spirit say, "We went to the Super Bowl because we avoided injury, but this year no Super Bowl."

Within the first two minutes our all-star receiver Steve Smith left the game with a season ending injury. By the end of the first quarter two more starters were out for the season. By the time we had played three games, we had lost thirteen players on both offense and defense to season ending injuries.

There was no trip to the Super Bowl that year for the Carolina Panthers. We didn't even go to the playoffs.

What's this about? Is God a Panther fan? Does He even care about a football game? No. But, again, this is about learning to hear God's voice in the little things so that we are prepared to hear His still small voice in the Day of Jacob's when survival is everything. **Your point!?**

I have found that the first rule of hearing God's voice is to ask! Ask! Ask! Ask to enter His training.

Chapter Twenty-One

Don't Get Fanatical!

"You have to keep a balance," she said.

"You don't want to become so heavenly minded that you're of no earthly good," said another.

How many times have you heard that one?

Who is the unbalanced one? Is it the person who is earth minded like the chicken that keeps looking at the ground and pecking at the dirt so it can eat some dirty seeds for dinner in its enclosed barnyard? Or, is it the eagle that lives in the high places, that can look into the sun (Son) and can still spot a fish in the river below?

Who's unbalanced? Is it the unregenerate one who seeks their destiny and satisfaction here in a world system that is dying? Or, is it the Spirit-filled individual who has been endowed with spiritual gifts given to them to assist them in taking dominion of the earth?

Okay, I admit it! I have had my love of this world burned out of me and it seems like I'm of no earthly good. I haven't kept up with the latest styles and new technologies and I work a manual labor job for low class money. But looks are deceiving. My spiritual orientation gives me power over earthly things so I can stand in the evil day when desperation abounds.

Adam was balanced before the curse when He had daily

fellowship with God. He had a vertical relationship and used what He gained from it to take dominion on the horizontal plane. The fall took away much of that vertical relationship when heaven and earth were in balance. *That* was normal. *That* is what will be restored to us at His coming. *That* is the type of balance I want.

What are you?

Are you a human being trying to have a spiritual experience or a spiritual being enduring a human experience in this world?

I have often been asked, "Where are you from?" As I become more conformed to His image I stumble at this question. Sometimes I make a joke and say, "Hmmm, is that a metaphysical question?" I can either answer, "Mike from Milwaukee," or "I'm a messenger sent from God to prepare the nations for the Day of Trouble and the Coming of Jesus. The Lord has sent me to stir you up and navigate you to the Lord."

On the question of fanaticism, I recall that someone once said, "Zeal in defense of the Truth is no sin."

Chapter Twenty-Two

The Pastor's Conference

In my dream I was attending a pastor's conference where there were over one thousand well-known and famous ministers. I was a young man just ordained and this was my first pastor's conference.

I walked into this luxurious and ornate conference hall and saw all the big named ministers standing around waiting to be seated. They all had their name tags and were talking amongst themselves and exchanging ministry cards and lining up their next speaking engagements. Then, Jesus walked in and He was invisible to everyone but me. He came up to me and whispered in my ear, "Don't speak until I say so." I realized He was telling me to keep silent while the established ones were trying to line up speaking tours so they could tell everything they know and earn a living. I realized they could speak feely but *I had to be quiet.* O, Lord, why? That's not fair!

Jesus proceeded to go around to about twenty other young ministers and whispered the same thing in their ears, "Don't speak until I say so." I felt better knowing that I was not the only one told to be quiet. Misery loves company you know? After all, I'm supposed to be out there saving people and giving the words of life to them. I thought, "You called me to be a minister but you won't let me do that!" and gave a growl of disgust.

When Jesus had completed speaking to us twenty "gagged ones," He went to the staircase and went up to the second floor balcony and looked back at us and said in a mind-to-mind communication: *"If you want what I want for you, you can't have what they want. They are the priests of the old order and it is a part realm. You have asked for the fullness and that is reserved for the very end. Then you will be released, but the old must die out first, just as King Saul died so that David could come forth."*

This dream drove me to study all the times of silence mentioned in Scripture, where God took His messengers off the scene and hid them, just before the cataclysmic event took place, in order to protect them.

God was making it clear that the present order of priests were doing a good thing that has brought us to this point. They have done well, but they will still protect their territory and not release the Davidic Company that now waits in the "wilderness."

With that said, there is a God in heaven and He has sent you into this world on a mission. He is closely monitoring your steps. He needs your attention and obedience to accomplish the good thing He has begun in you. All hell is about to break out on this planet and He needs a people that will listen, hear, and take orders.

Your survival is at stake.

Chapter Twenty-Three

God's Curriculum

When you are called to be a prophetic teacher, and by that I mean…

- You are called to teach Biblical principles vital to the needs of the church and its members to raise up a standard and prepare them for what is to come, and

- Things like anomalies and confirmations happen as a witness to validate you and your message

…God will order your steps in relation to what you are to study and when and in what order.

My testimony is that my Father – the greatest father and teacher who ever lived – has done just that in my life over some thirty-five years. So, let share with you the journey He put me on as He directed my studies, preparing me to be used to warn, prepare, and equip His faithful remnant who will,

- Stand before the evil forces of an antichrist system and speak God's indictments and warnings to those who are the enemies of God, and

- Be the "carriers" of the fullness of the Spirit and minister to hurting and desperate people in the coming "day that burns like an oven."

The following is a list of word studies and prophetic

directions given to me by the Lord so that I would know what He wanted me to know. In it I have seen over the years that He spoke to me certain words to direct me on a specific path to understanding His overall plan for these days at the close of this age. These promptings came over decades. In the beginning, I did not understand or see that He was spoon feeding me specific concepts that were connecting the dots of seemingly unrelated Biblical principles. Only after two decades did I see the pattern and that all the side studies had a specific purpose in mind that would allow me to connect seemingly unrelated ideas. My steps were ordered in what I was to study and this shows that these studies were not just me with a wild imagination or soulish thirst for idle knowledge. There was a pattern to this journey and it can and should be the same for you if you are being groomed for something in the future.

These revelations changed my life and made me into a prophetic teacher, bringing to the surface Biblical principles that the church was not addressing or facing and it is my destiny to bring the Body of Christ into remembrance of these forgotten things. With that said, here is what He had me study:

1. *"The remnant"* -- In the beginning of my Christian life back in the late 1970's I was reading about how Solomon asked God for wisdom to lead His people. I was a "wannabe" back then, so I too asked for wisdom, knowledge, and discernment. Shortly after, I heard a voice say to me, *"Study the remnant."* I had previously

come to know how to do detailed and organized word studies and why they were so important. I also came to see how speaking a word in your ear was a common way God functioned with those who thirsted after truth and went after it aggressively. After I heard the word "remnant," I went to my Strong's Concordance and started compiling the passages on the word "remnant." This part of the study taught me that out of the entire community of believers, *only a remnant* will survive in the evil day. As I continued in this study, reading every passage where "remnant" was mentioned, I also began to notice that several other words were often connected to this word "remnant." This study, initiated by the Holy Spirit when I heard the word "remnant," allowed me to connect the dots of obscure passages and see deeper into the overall plan of God in the Scriptures. Without an understanding of God's plan for mankind, through a separated priesthood called Israel, you will be just like a chicken on a farm walking through life pecking in the dirt for a morsel here and a morsel there and never have an understanding of the day you are living in. Without this understanding you will also fall for "any wind of doctrine," and be "unskillful in dividing the word of truth," making you a "double-minded man."

2. *"Afflicted," "scattered,"* and *"regathered"* -- I put these together and learned that God will have an *"afflicted,*

scattered, and regathered remnant." But it didn't end there. This study has expanded and uncovered a major principle in scripture that the masses of the church have never seen or heard. The reason many haven't seen it is either because they are not hungry for truth and aren't driven to plumb the depths of God's Word, thereby remaining in darkness, or they rely on the preacher or Sunday school teacher to feed them. This is an entitlement mentality where people rely on others for everything. This type of lifestyle will never be blessed and they that live that way will never experience an open heaven over their lives. After further study these words also became connected to the words,

3. *"Israel"* and *"sifted"* – God's *"afflicted, scattered, and regathered remnant"* was spoken of as being *"sifted amongst the nations."* The word driven is sometimes used. The meaning is that God will drive and scatter His people into the nations ("wilderness") of the Gentiles and there they will be afflicted and in their afflictions they will consider who they are and what their destiny is as "kings and priests" and "stewards of the mysteries." Do you see how this describes that scattered Israel will have their eyes opened in the wilderness and as a result come under the New Covenant?

4. *"Hide, hid, hiding, and hidden"* -- As I did what the Holy Spirit prescribed, I learned that the word "hide" was also

connected to the word "until" – this gave me understanding of what He was trying to reveal to me for *this hour*. This study built on the previous study and it is plain to see that God was connecting the dots for me. This study was truly not of my doing. All I needed to do was do what I was guided to do. I had to expend the energy to be blessed with understanding. After I exhausted all the references to "*hide*," "*hid*," "*hiding*," and "*hidden*," I saw that God has had and will have a remnant that He has hidden until an...

5. "*Appointed time*," or "*time appointed*" -- This was another phrase connected to this Spirit-led journey. Preterists teach that the "time of the end" was this "appointed time" and it occurred at the fall of Jerusalem in 70A.D. This a very true application but it has a double reference as many end time prophecies have. I was led to Revelation 10:6-7 where it says that "*time is no longer*" and refers to the end of Daniel's time-cycle prophecies of 2300, 2520, 1260, 1290, and 1335 years (If these numbers intrigue you, see my contact information at the end of this book.). I realized that if you don't know who Israel is, and the time cycles of prophecies where God dealt with them in certain ways, you will be confused in your understanding of end time prophecy and what God is doing and when.

6. "*Appointed place*—The is a very revealing concept from

Chronicles and Samuel. I ask, where is the "appointed place?" You have probably been taught that it the land of Palestine in the Middle East. You would be half right because there is also a second "appointed place" and it will surprise you I am sure but that is a topic for another book.

7. *"Midnight"* -- Again, I got out my concordance and went through every passage that mentioned "midnight." As I got further into the study, I heard Him say, *"Study the things that happened at midnight, for in them you will see what I am going to do at the time of the change, how I will do it, and when."* Well, you can see that *that* was a very detailed instruction and the study revealed just what He said it would. When you have been shown these details of how God will bring the judgments upon the earth and what the result will be, you are rewarded for your effort with the "peace that surpasses all understanding." In my daily life now, I don't experience what I see many experiencing all around me: worry, panic, fear, emotional imbalance, ill-logic, torment, anguish, or self-destructive behavior. I see what people do to mask their true inner feelings and when you mask too much for too long one runs the risk of imbalance.

8. "Glory" -- Contrary to what we have been taught, God will share His glory with another. Namely us! God told Moses that He would make Moses *like a God* to the

people, and the scripture teaches us that God will give us glory and show His glory through us! Is that not exciting? If the theology that you have been taught differs with this, change your theology. It is amazing what we can learn when we study the Word thoroughly and within the scope of the entire Bible from Genesis to Revelation, rather than simply listening to a preacher teach you one or two hours a week. He did the study and hopefully experienced the Divine leading that led him on his journey, but what did you get? Your ears were tickled, yet very little stuck to your subconscious mind. Remember, God showed Israel His *acts*, but to Moses He showed His *ways*. I would rather be God's friend and know *why* He did what He did rather than just see *what* He did. He showed Moses *both* His acts and ways because Moses became His friend!

9. *The two houses of Israel, the lost ten tribes of Israel*, and *the identity of the two witnesses* -- The history backing the principles of the two houses, the lost tribes, and the two witnesses is so vast that I cannot begin to explain it at this time. Yet, when these revelations were grasped, the Bible opened up in a greater way and I was given a great understanding of end time prophecy and the timing of end time events.

These are just a few of the words and concepts that God spoke to me DIRECTLY to study over 30 plus years. My studies did not come from my preconceived desires to know stuff. I do have that but and that drive is essential for those who will be in the five fold ministry. You are BORN WITH THAT. When your spirit gets regenerated, God takes your natural gifts and desires and throws fuel on it and begins to DIVINELY ORDER what you are to study because He has a specific ministry for you to become a specialist in. For me its the apocalyptic studies and both secular and ecclesiastical histories.

There are many deceptions out there in the world and in the church and without a Spirit-led curriculum where God comes to you and tells you what to study, you'll never come to know what God is doing and when He is doing it. This ignorance could get you killed in the times ahead.

God will often get you started off by speaking "a word behind you," and then once you get rolling you will run across other words and principles that lead you to a revelation that brings you a sense of awe. God was taking me on a journey in His word and this "revelation journey" was brought to me by none other than the Word Himself. He has been my tour guide. It felt like I was watching a music director conducting a symphony or like watching one of those old time pianos where the keys move and plays music without a pianist. I could see the keys being pushed. All I had to do was follow the conductor. I could see I was being personally led by the Holy Spirit to a divine revelation into a major concept in Scripture that most Christians knew and still know nothing about. And frankly, without this revelation, no one can qualify to be a part of the end time apostolic company that will raise a standard and clarify what Father is really doing. The coming company of apostles and prophets cannot be ignorant or confused over this concept of an *"afflicted, scattered, and regathered remnant that is hidden until an appointed time."*

If you will use that statement as your jumping off point to a thorough study, you will be lifted out of the "elementary doctrines" into the deeper layers of the onion and you will be granted a graduation gift! That graduation gift that you will get, because you will have made a quantum leap in your understanding of God's plan for mankind, will be what the Bible calls *"the tongue of the learned."*

When you make that quantum leap in your understanding, because you paid a price to search out the scriptures for the "treasure hidden in a field," you will walk and talk differently. People will notice it even when you don't think there is anything special to see. That's the way it is. There will be authority in your voice and it will be said of you what was said of me,

"Mike Killion hears from God."

"When Mike opens his mouth, profound things come out."

"When Mike speaks, everybody listens."

"There's a man with a lot of jewels."

I'm writing this so that you will hopefully see that you too are on this scripted journey and see Him more fully.

About the author

I was born in Tampa, Florida in 1947 and grew up in South Milwaukee, Wisconsin. I studied fine arts and education at the University of Wisconsin-Milwaukee where I received my Bachelor of Fine Arts with teacher certification in 1973. I was regenerated to life in Christ shortly after when I read the sinner's prayer in the back of Hal Lindsey's book *The Late Great Planet Earth*.

After I was converted I was given the gift of hunger for God's word and I asked for two things:

1. Wisdom, knowledge, and discernment in the things of God, and
2. That God would show me things that ministers had either forgotten or were ignoring due to denominational restrictions.

I wanted to know the hidden things not being spoken of. I believed that true messengers of God were duty bound to "tell it like it is" with no reservations or apologies, regardless of whether the church was ready for it. I observed in the scriptures that people are never ready for a move of God and they must "deal with it." We must conform to God, not the other way around.

I also made this covenant with the Lord: "*I will go anywhere you want me to go, do anything you want me to do, say anything you want me to say, to whomever you want me to say it, and I will not be afraid of their faces."*

This is when God took over and began to drive my life on the road to my processing. Like a blind man, stumbling through the forest, I didn't know where I was going but I knew God was leading and not wasting any time. The hunger He gave me often had me reading four or five books at a time. Behind every trial and test there was a revelation of truth that had to be burned into me by experience, taking me beyond mere theory. My struggle was not between right and wrong but between my "good" ideas and His will.

Along the way, God said this to me: *"You have asked for the High Calling, the apprehended life, and all I have for you. To get caught up in a career or a professional ministry will only slow you down and you'll camp there and miss the best ministry which comes at the end."* At this time I had no knowledge of the "hidden ones" and the "times of silence," imposed upon messengers of the next move of God.

My freedom from religious entanglements, coupled with this insatiable, God-given hunger, has given me unique insights into things not spoken of in churches today. My freedom from men and budgets have given me the boldness to speak openly and prick the minds of the saints.

God has pulled me into studies on the Bible, Biblical and secular history, anthropology and archaeology, the rise and fall of nations, end-time prophecy, conspiracy theories, science, and current events. My ministry consists of writing educational and prophetic articles, along with spiritual counseling and dream interpretation.

I am single, semi-retired (working part-time), and living with my youngest son Tyler in Charlotte, North Carolina. I presently attend two churches: Antioch International Church and Morningstar Fellowship Church, both of which are in Fort Mill, South Carolina.

I also am a degreed, accomplished, award-winning painter and mural artist with a collection of fifty paintings.

The name of my ministry is *The Navigator Prophetic Ministry*. I chose this name because I saw myself as a sign post along the way pointing the way to the hidden treasures and the next move of God.

I believe that your identity among men is not determined by yourself but by seasoned five-fold ministers that speak over you along the way. Those who have spoken into my life have given me several nicknames:

"The stick that stirs the drink" -- I stir people to consider things they may have neglected to consider. It is my objective to stimulate people to dig for deeper truths.

"The cattle prod"

"The oasis in the desert" -- People, who are searching for clarity and peace, are drawn to me.

Contact Information

Mike Killion

The Navigator Prophetic Ministry

e-Mail: NavMike8@gmail.com

Mobile: 704-299-1580

www.ingramcontent.com/pod-product-compliance
Lightning Source LLC
Chambersburg PA
CBHW030949090426
42737CB00007B/557